FAMOUS LIVES

Campaigners for Change

Rosemary Moore

WAYLAND

FAMOUS LIVES

Kings and Queens
Saints
Inventors
Explorers
Artists
Engineers
Writers
Campaigners for Change

Series Editor: Alex Woolf
Book Editor: Liz Harman
Designer: Joyce Chester
Consultant: Norah Granger

First published in 1997 by Wayland (Publishers) Limited,
61 Western Road, Hove, East Sussex, BN3 1JD

Find Wayland on the internet at http://www.wayland.co.uk

British Library Cataloguing in Publication Data

Moore, Rosemary, 1928–
Campaigners for change. – (Famous lives)
1. Political activists – Biography – Juvenile literature
2. Women political activists – Biography – Juvenile
literature 3. Human rights workers – Biography –
Juvenile literature 4. Women human rights workers –
Biography – Juvenile literature
I. Title
323.1'0922

ISBN 0 7502 2105 4

Typeset by Joyce Chester
Printed by L.E.G.O. S.p.A., Vicenza, Italy

Picture Acknowledgements

The publishers would like to thank the following for allowing
their pictures to be used in this book: Associated
Press/Topham 15, 22; Camera Press 5, 19, 24, 28 (bottom
left); Mary Evans 4, 12; Mary Evans/Fawcett Library 8; Mary
Evans/Photo Researchers USA 16; John Frost Newspapers
cover (background) and 2–3 (background); Hulton Getty title
page and 10 and 28 (bottom right), 10 (bottom), 11 (both),
18 and 29 (top), 20 and 29 (middle); Panos Pictures 21, 25;
Popperfoto cover (right) and page 28 (top), 9, 13, 14, 15
(top), 17, 26 and 29 (bottom), 27; Topham Picturepoint
cover (bottom left), 6, 7; Rex Features 23; Wayland Picture
Library cover (top left)

Contents

Florence Nightingale

Florence Nightingale grew up in the reign of Queen Victoria (1837–1901). The Nightingale family was wealthy and Florence's parents hoped their daughter would marry a rich man. However, Florence had other ideas.

Florence visited hospitals. Her parents did not approve. In those days, hospitals were dirty, gloomy places. Most nurses were not properly trained. Florence wanted to make hospitals better places for sick people.

Nurses looking after wounded soldiers on a battlefield during the Crimean War. ▽

Far away, the Crimean War was being fought between British and Russian soldiers. Florence heard about the dreadful army hospitals, where thousands of wounded men were dying from hunger and lack of care. She decided to take a group of nurses to the war area, to care for the wounded soldiers.

DATES

1820 Birth of Florence Nightingale
1854 Florence Nightingale goes to Turkey to nurse wounded soldiers
1910 Death of Florence Nightingale

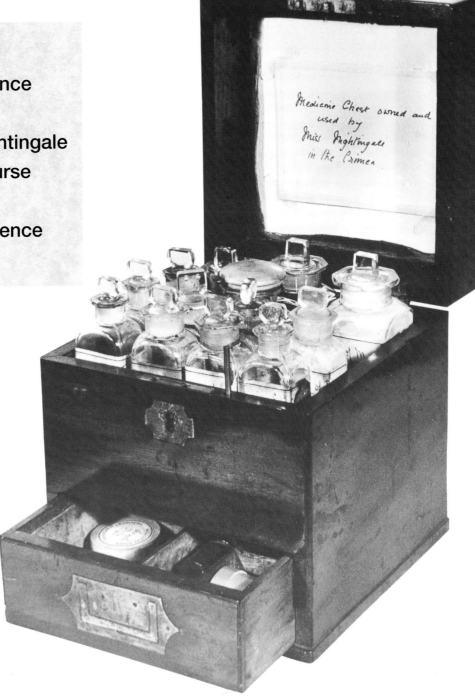

Florence took this box of medicines with her to use during the Crimean War. ▷

Medicine Chest owned and used by Miss Nightingale in the Crimea.

When Florence and her nurses arrived in the war area, they found injured men lying in dirty rooms. Rats ran over their beds. Florence arranged for the hospital to be cleaned and for food and medicines to be brought in.

Florence was kind to the soldiers and looked after them. They all loved her. At night, Florence walked with her lamp through the dark wards (rooms), comforting the men. They called her 'The Lady of the Lamp'.

Florence Nightingale and her nurses caring for wounded soldiers at the hospital during the Crimean War. ▽

△ *Florence Nightingale (sitting in the middle of the group) was an old lady when this picture was taken, showing her with nurses from St Thomas's Hospital.*

When Florence returned to England, she started a school to train nurses at St Thomas's Hospital in London. The nurses wore uniforms and Florence taught them how to care for sick people. She made strict rules about how to run the hospital and keep it clean.

Modern hospitals and nursing methods are based on Florence Nightingale's work.

Emmeline Pankhurst

Emmeline Goulden grew up in Victorian England, when women had no say in who governed them. Because she was a girl, she was expected to stay at home and was not given the same education as her brothers.

When Emmeline was 20 years old, she married Doctor Richard Pankhurst. Richard and Emmeline both thought that women, as well as men, should be allowed to vote for Members of Parliament (MPs) at elections.

DATES

1858 Birth of Emmeline Pankhurst

1918 Women over 30 allowed to vote

1928 Death of Emmeline Pankhurst

◁ *Emmeline Pankhurst at about the time she formed the suffragette movement.*

△ *Suffragettes and their supporters marching through London in 1908.*

After her husband's death, Emmeline formed a group with other women who wanted to be allowed to vote. They were called suffragettes. They protested at meetings and marched to Parliament. The MPs refused to listen.

Emmeline tried to talk to the Prime Minister. She wanted him to change the law so that women could vote. But she was arrested and sent to prison. This was the first of many times she went to prison.

Many suffragettes, including Emmeline's daughters, Christabel and Sylvia, went to prison. Sometimes they refused to eat. Then the prison warders forced food through rubber tubes down their throats. When the women became ill they were sent home. When they had recovered, they were sent back to prison again.

◁ *Emmeline Pankhurst and her daughter Christabel dressed in prison clothes.*

During the First World War (1914–18), many men went away to fight. Women took their places and did the jobs that men had done, like working on farms and in factories. The war changed women's lives completely. For four years they had been doing men's work. Their rights could no longer be ignored.

Women working in a factory during the First World War. ▷

In 1918, women over the age of 30 were allowed to vote for the first time. In 1928, just before Emmeline died, women were at last given the same voting rights as men.

A woman voting in an election in 1918. For the first time, women over the age of 30 were allowed to vote. ▽

Mohandas Gandhi

Mohandas Gandhi grew up in India at a time when the country was ruled by Britain. He was a clever boy who studied to become a lawyer. After passing his exams, he went to work in South Africa. There he helped other Indians to protest against unfair treatment by the South African Government.

Many British people lived in India and made the laws. They lived very comfortable lives and had Indian servants. ▽

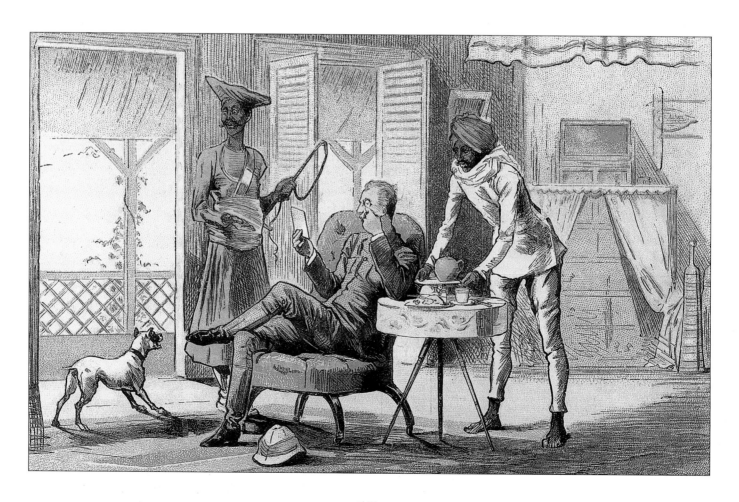

Gandhi as a young man, when he was studying law. ▷

Gandhi returned to India in 1915. Like many Indians, Gandhi wanted India to be free from British rule. He told Indian people to protest against the British by calmly disobeying unfair laws, and quietly accepting punishment for their actions. Huge numbers of Indians followed his advice. Gandhi called for everybody to stop work as a protest. The British punished the workers and Gandhi was horrified by the violence.

The British put Gandhi in prison for six years. When he was released, he carried on organizing peaceful protests. He was sent to prison again for many years.

13

△ *During the 1930s, Gandhi visited Britain several times for talks about what was happening in India. This picture shows Gandhi being greeted as he arrives in London in 1931.*

Gandhi's followers called him 'Mahatma', meaning 'Great Soul'. He inspired millions of Indians to oppose their rulers and stand up to them peacefully and bravely. At last, in 1947, British rule in India ended and the country became independent. But independence was followed by terrible fighting between people of the Hindu religion and people who were Moslems.

Gandhi with his granddaughters. ▷

This violence made Gandhi very unhappy. As a protest against the killing and bloodshed, he fasted (stopped eating). Most of the Indian people loved Gandhi for what he had done for them. They did not want him to die so they stopped the fighting. Sadly, a few months later, Gandhi was murdered by an angry Hindu man.

People visiting the place where Gandhi's body was cremated in 1948. ▷

Martin Luther King

Sixty years ago, in the southern USA, a young black boy called Martin Luther King was growing up. As he grew older, Martin saw how badly black Americans were treated by white Americans. Blacks could not attend the same schools, eat in the same restaurants or travel on the same buses as whites.

△ *In the 1950s and '60s, many shops in the south of the USA had signs saying that only white people were allowed in.*

Martin became a minister (priest) in the Baptist Church. He studied in Boston, in the northern USA, where he saw that life was much better for black Americans.

Martin Luther King, who worked all his life to gain equality for black Americans ▷

When he returned to the south, Martin decided to try to get equal treatment for blacks. He told them they had the right to be treated the same as whites. When a black woman was arrested for refusing to give up her bus seat to a white man, Martin told blacks that they should refuse to travel on buses. And he joined college students who were protesting against the separation of blacks and whites in cafés.

17

All over the south, Martin Luther King led peaceful protests, calling for equal rights for black people. In 1963 he led thousands of people, both black and white, on a march to Washington, the capital of the USA. In a speech he said: 'I have a dream, that my four little children will be judged not by the colour of their skin, but by the content of their character'.

Martin Luther King speaking to the huge crowd at the end of the march to Washington in 1963. ▽

Martin Luther King and his wife and children hold hands as they pray around the dinner table. ▽

Martin Luther King had many enemies. In 1968 he was shot and killed by a white man. Although life for many black Americans has improved, they have still not gained complete equality, for which Martin Luther King fought so hard.

Mother Teresa

Agnes Bojaxhiu was born in Macedonia, near Greece. When she was 18 years old, Agnes became a Catholic nun, taking the name of Teresa. She was sent to Calcutta in India, where she became a teacher in a school for rich Catholic girls.

Outside the garden walls of the school was a very different world. In Calcutta, thousands of starving people had no homes and lived on the city's streets.

DATES

1910 Birth of Mother Teresa
1950 Mother Teresa founds The Missionaries of Charity
1979 Mother Teresa is given the Nobel Peace Prize for her work for the poor people of the world

Mother Teresa on a visit to Paris, France in 1965. ▷

Teresa believed that she had to leave her comfortable life and help these people, bringing them food, medical care and love.

Teresa asked the Catholic Church for permission to go into the streets to work among the poor. She learnt to speak the local language, Bengali, and to care for the sick.

△ *Some of Mother Teresa's helpers serving a meal at a home for the poor in Calcutta.*

The Church gave Teresa permission to found a religious group, called the Missionaries of Charity. The Missionaries began by opening a small school in the Calcutta slums and giving sick and hungry people medicine and food.

Soon, the Missionaries opened shelters for the poor and homeless, and special homes to care for old, sick and dying people. Later, a group of Missionary Brothers was formed.

◁ *Mother Teresa travels all over the world trying to help people. This picture shows her on a visit to Romania in 1990.*

Today, the Missionaries of Charity care for people in cities all over the world, including the poor and homeless in Britain and the USA. But their greatest work is still among the 'poorest of the poor' people of Calcutta.

Mother Teresa meets children all over the world. She teaches them to 'meet each other with a smile, for a smile is the beginning of love.' ▽

Nelson Mandela

Nelson Mandela grew up in a South African village. His parents called him Xhosa, which means 'stirring up trouble'. It was a good name for him!

When he grew up, Nelson went to Johannesburg to study to become a lawyer. There, he saw that black people were very unfairly treated by white people. He joined the African National Congress (ANC), a group that worked for the rights of black South Africans.

DATES

1918 Birth of Nelson Mandela
1990 Nelson Mandela is released from prison
1994 Nelson Mandela elected President of the Republic of South Africa

As a young man, Nelson Mandela worked for equality for black people in South Africa. ▷

Many black people in South Africa have spent all their lives living in poor townships like this. ▷

Nelson and his friends protested against the new 'apartheid' laws in South Africa, which separated people because of the colour of their skin. Under apartheid, blacks were forced to live away from the big towns, in poor, shabby townships, and work for whites for very low wages.

It was against the law for members of the ANC to meet, but Nelson Mandela carried on working secretly for the ANC. The Police found out and he was arrested and sent to prison.

Nelson spent 28 years in prison. For much of the time, he was alone in his cell. Other countries of the world did not approve of the apartheid laws and called for the South African Government to free Nelson Mandela. At last, on 11 February 1990, at the age of 72, Nelson was finally released from prison.

△ *With his wife Winnie, Nelson Mandela waves to the crowds after he is released from the prison where he was held for 28 years.*

The South African President, F. W. de Klerk, asked Nelson Mandela to help plan for black South Africans to rule their country. Four years after Nelson left prison, all South Africans, black and white, voted to elect a new President. Mandela became the first black President of the Republic of South Africa.

Nelson Mandela arriving at the South African Parliament. The man on the right is F. W. de Klerk, whom he replaced as President. ▽

Timeline

Year	Campaigner	How long ago?
1820	Florence Nightingale born in Florence, Italy	180 years ago
1830		170 years ago
1840		160 years ago
1850		150 years ago
1854	Florence Nightingale leads a group of nurses to Scutari in Turkey	
1858	Emmeline Pankhurst born	
1860	Florence Nightingale opens a training school for nurses at Saint Thomas's Hospital, London	140 years ago
1869	Mohandas Gandhi born at Porbandar, India	
1870		130 years ago
1880		120 years ago
1890		110 years ago
1900		100 years ago
1910	Death of Florence Nightingale	90 years ago
1910	Mother Teresa born in Skopje, Macedonia	
1918	Women over the age of 30 get the vote	
1918	Nelson Mandela born in Transkei region of South Africa	
1919	Gandhi organizes a peaceful protest against British rule	
1920		80 years ago

Year	Campaigner	How long ago?
1920		80 years ago
1928	Death of Emmeline Pankhurst	
1929	Martin Luther King born in Atlanta, Georgia, USA	
1930		70 years ago
1940		60 years ago
1946	Mother Teresa decides she must care for the people of Calcutta's slums	
1947	India becomes independent	
1948	Gandhi murdered	
1950		50 years ago
1956	Martin Luther King leads a protest to stop people using buses in Montgomery, Alabama	
1960		40 years ago
1962	Nelson Mandela sentenced to 5 years in prison	
1964	Nelson Mandela sent to prison for life	
1968	Martin Luther King murdered	
1970		30 years ago
1979	Mother Teresa is awarded the Nobel Peace Prize	
1980		20 years ago
1990	Nelson Mandela set free	10 years ago
1994	Nelson Mandela elected President of the Republic of South Africa	

Words to look up

African National Congress (ANC) an organization formed to gain freedom for black South Africans

apartheid a law in South Africa that kept people of different races apart

Catholic Church the branch of the Christian religion led by the Pope

cell a very small room

cremated burned to ashes

elections votes in which people choose who will represent them

equality being equal and having the same rights as everyone else

government a group of people who rule a country

Hindu following the Hindu religion, the main religion in India

independent free from the control of another country

lawyer someone who studies the law

Members of Parliament (MPs) men and women who have been elected to sit in the House of Commons, one of the two Houses of Parliament in London

missionaries people who do religious work and help the poor and sick all over the world

Moslems people who follow the religion of Islam

Nobel Peace Prize a prize awarded to people who have worked very hard to achieve world peace

nun a woman who lives with a group of other women of the same religion, who follow certain rules

organization a large group of people working together for a purpose

parliament a place where MPs meet to make laws and govern a country

President a person who is in charge of a republic

Prime Minister the leader of the British Government

protest a demonstration of disapproval or disagreement

republic a place where the people elect their political representatives

rights the ability to expect fair treatment

slums places where poor people live in overcrowded conditions

suffragettes women in Britain in the early twentieth century who fought to obtain the right to vote

townships areas of housing set aside for black people

vote a person's opinion or choice, especially during an election

warders people who guard prisoners in prison

Other books to look at

Famous Campaigners for Change by Nina Morgan, Wayland, 1993

Florence Nightingale by Nina Morgan, Wayland, 1992

Florence Nightingale by Richard Tame, Franklin Watts, 1989

Gandhi by Peggy Burns, Wayland, 1993

Gandhi by Brenda Clarke, Cherrytree, 1988

Martin Luther King by Nina Morgan, Wayland, 1993

Mother Teresa by Joan Graff Clucas, Harrap, 1990

Mother Teresa by Wayne Jackman, Wayland, 1993

Nelson Mandela by Richard Tames, Franklin Watts, 1991

Nelson Mandela by Richard Killeen, Wayland, 1995

Women at War by A. Susan Williams, Wayland, 1989

Some places to see

The Florence Nightingale Museum, 2 Lambeth Palace Road, London – a museum at St Thomas's Hospital, with exhibitions about Florence Nightingale and the Nursing School at Saint Thomas's Hospital

The Pankhurst Centre, 60–62 Nelson Street, Chorton-on-Medlock, Manchester – the home of Emmeline Pankhurst, which now houses exhibitions relating to the history of the struggle of British women to win the vote.

Index